ABSOLUTE BEGINNERS
Harmonica

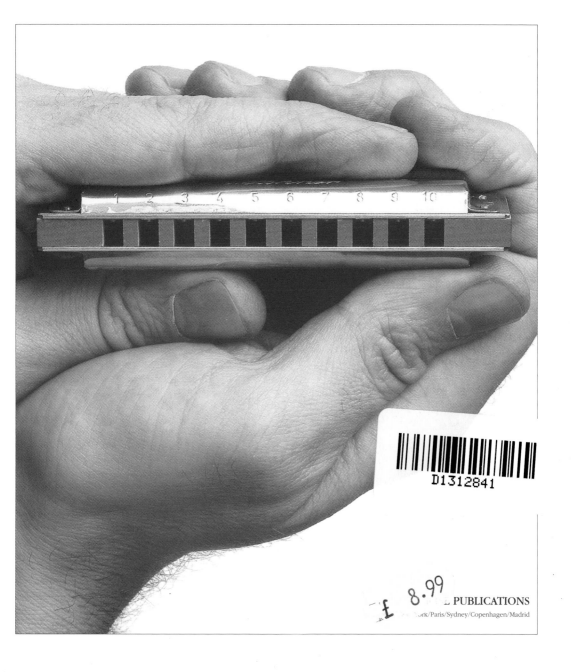

£ 8.99

PUBLICATIONS

...ork/Paris/Sydney/Copenhagen/Madrid

D1312841

Exclusive Distributors:
Music Sales Limited
14-15 Berners Street,
London W1T 3LJ, UK.

Music Sales Corporation
257 Park Avenue South,
New York,
NY 10010, USA

Music Sales Pty Limited
20 Resolution Drive,
Caringbah, NSW 2229,
Australia.

Order No. AM970618
ISBN 0-7119-8893-5
This book © Copyright 2001 by Wise Publications
in association with Omnibus Press
www.musicsales.com

Unauthorised reproduction of any part of this publication by any
means including photocopying is an infringement of copyright.

Written by Steve Jennings.
Photographs by George Taylor.
Book design by Chloë Alexander.
Model: Andrew King.
Instruments kindly loaned by Hanks.

Printed in the United Kingdom by Printwise Limited,
Haverhill, Suffolk.

Your Guarantee of Quality:
As publishers, we strive to produce every book to the highest
commercial standards. This book has been carefully designed to
minimise awkward page turns and to make playing from it a real
pleasure. Particular care has been given to specifying acid-free,
neutral-sized paper made from pulps which have not been
elemental chlorine bleached. This pulp is from farmed sustainable
forests and was produced with special regard for the environment.
Throughout, the printing and binding have been planned to
ensure a sturdy, attractive publication which should give years of
enjoyment. If your copy fails to meet our high standards, please
inform us and we will gladly replace it.

Contents

Introduction

Welcome to Absolute Beginners for Harmonica. The harmonica is one of the most popular instruments in the world – this book will guide you from the very first time you pick up your harmonica right through to playing some of the world's best loved melodies.

Easy-to-follow instructions
will guide you through

- reading harmonica notation
- playing chords and single notes
- playing your first song

Play along with the backing track as you learn – the specially recorded CD will let you hear how the music *should* sound – then try playing the part yourself.

Practice regularly and often. Twenty minutes every day is far better than two hours at the weekend with nothing in between. Not only are you training your brain to understand how to play the harmonica, you are also teaching your muscles to memorise certain repeated actions.

At the back of this book you will find a section introducing some of the music available for the harmonica. It will guide you to exactly the kind of music you want to play – whether it's a comprehensive tutorial series, rock licks, jazz and blues, easy-to-play tunes or "off the record" transcriptions, there's something there for all tastes.

Bluesmaster

Meisterklasse

Lee Oskar

Which harp?

Blues Harp

What sort of harmonica do I need?

For this book you'll need what is known as a 10 hole Richter tuned major diatonic harmonica in the key of C (phew!).

Most players refer to this as a C *harp*. C harps are marketed under a variety of names, such as Bluesmaster, Meisterklasse, Pocket Pal, Easy Rider, Blues Harp, Major Boy, Marine Band, Lee Oskar, Golden Melody, Silvertone, Super 20, Star Performer, Folk Master, Folk Blues, Big River Harp, Pro Harp and Cross Harp, and many more.

Essentially, these are all the same thing, though prices and quality (and even shapes!) can vary. Just make sure that the instrument you are using has a single row of 10 holes and is marked with the letter C and you shouldn't go too far wrong.

Marine Band case

Marine Band

Pro Harp

Getting started

Before blowing your first notes, here are a few simple points about music and how it's written.

Music is notated on five equally spaced lines called a *stave* (or staff):

The squiggly thing at the beginning of the stave is known as a *treble clef.* There are other clefs, but for our purposes this is the only one you need to know. The position of notes on the lines and spaces of the stave, or above and below it, shows you their *pitch*.

All musical sounds or notes have pitches – how low or how high they happen to be. The notes also have names taken from the first seven letters of the alphabet:

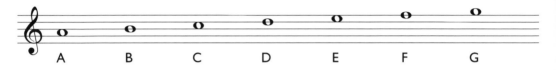

A   B   C   D   E   F   G

After G, we start again at A. This is because although the second A is "higher" than the first one, they sound very similar, and also because if each individual pitch had a unique name you'd need to have a memory like a computer to retain them all – whereas the alphabet you already know!

Jargon Buster

Pitch – how high or low a note is
Stave – the 5 lines on which music is written
Clef – sign at the start of the stave that tells you which notes correspond to which pitches

The stave is divided into *bars* (or measures) by the use of vertical bar lines:

↑
bar line

↑
double
bar line

Each bar has a fixed number of *beats* in it. A beat is the natural tapping rhythm of a song – when you tap your foot to a piece of music you're responding to the beat. Most tunes have four beats in a bar, so you would count and/or tap your foot like this:

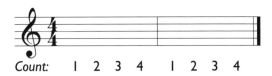

Count: 1 2 3 4   1 2 3 4

The two 4s set one above the other in the example above are what is called a *time signature*. The top number tells you how many beats there are in each bar – you don't need to worry about the bottom number for the time being.

As well as pitch, notes have *duration* – they last for a certain length of time. We'll introduce the different note durations as we go along. The first we're going to use is the semibreve, or whole note, which looks like this:

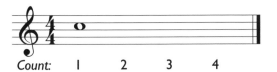

Count: 1   2   3   4

A semibreve lasts for four beats. Each type of note length has an equivalent *rest* to indicate that you remain silent for the same number of beats. A semibreve rest looks like this:

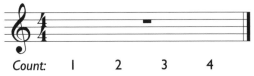

Count: 1   2   3   4

Jargon Buster

Beat – the natural pulse of music
Bar – groupings of regular numbers of beats
Time Signature – a sign at the start of the stave that tells you how many beats there are in each bar
Duration – how a long a note lasts
Rest – the opposite of a note; it tells you to remain silent for a certain number of beats

CHECKPOINT

WHAT YOU'VE ACHIEVED SO FAR...

You can now:
• Understand basic concepts of pitch, rhythm and counting

The first blow

Now it's time to play! Hold your harmonica between the thumb and forefinger of your left hand, with the soundholes facing you and the numbers uppermost, like this:

Now place your right hand like this:

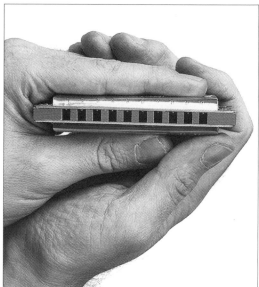

Raise the harmonica to your lips and gently exhale through it. Harmonica books talk about *blowing* and *drawing* the instrument. These are not the best terms because they imply a degree of force – harmonica playing should be relaxed and easy.

Try not to tense up too much; just breathe in and out through the instrument.

Tip
You may find it helps to imagine the sound you are producing as like a ping-pong ball supported on the column of air coming from your lungs, and if you blow too hard the ball will fall (but it won't break – stay relaxed!).

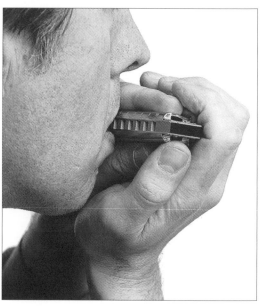

Blow for four

The first piece is titled "Blow For Four", because that's all you need to do – simply blow for four beats, then rest for four beats. Use any combination of blow notes anywhere on the harmonica, but remember not to play during the rests – it will sound awful if you do! The semibreve notes are only there to show you when to play – you choose which holes to use. Don't forget to count, as indicated, and notice that at the

end you play two chords (as two or more notes sounded together are called) in successive bars. Listen to **Track 1** to hear how it sounds. You will hear the drummer tapping the time for two bars before the band comes in – this is so that you know how fast your own counting should be.

Now try it yourself with **Track 2**.

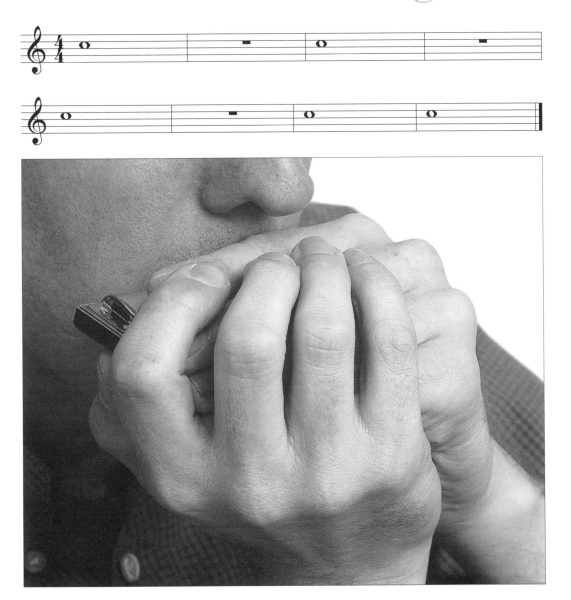

Finding notes

Now let's pick out some specific notes on your instrument.

To do this you need to know:
1 What specific notes look like in written music, and
2 What they look like in special harmonica tablature.

Bear in mind that while harmonica tablature is a way of making music-reading easier for you, it is not a substitute for reading music.

Locate hole 5 on your harmonica, either by using the tip of your tongue to 'count' up from hole 1, or by hand/eye co-ordination.

When you've "hit the spot", take your tongue away and blow hole 5 together with the two adjacent notes (4 and 6).

Listen carefully to **Track 3** and make sure that you're getting the same sound from your harmonica.

Notice that the hole numbers you need to play are stacked one above the other, like the musical notes they correspond to, and that in this example you see three plain numbers.

Plain numbers mean: blow that hole or combination of holes.

Next, try drawing, or sucking on, the same holes.

Remember that you should not be using force.
Just breathe in gently through your mouth – the reeds on the harmonica know what their purpose in life is, and they will respond to very little air pressure.
Again, listen carefully to **Track 4** and check that you're getting the same chord from your harmonica.

Notice that this time the numbers have circles round them and – you guessed it – circles mean draw on that hole or combination of holes.

The written music looks like this:

With the TAB (tablature) it looks like this:

The written music looks like this:

And with the TAB:

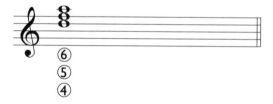

Blow for four, suck for more

When you're sure that you're matching the sounds I'm making on the CD, have a go at this little piece, which is a development of "Blow For Four", entitled

"Blow For Four, Suck For More". Listen to **Track 5** and then play along with **Track 6**.

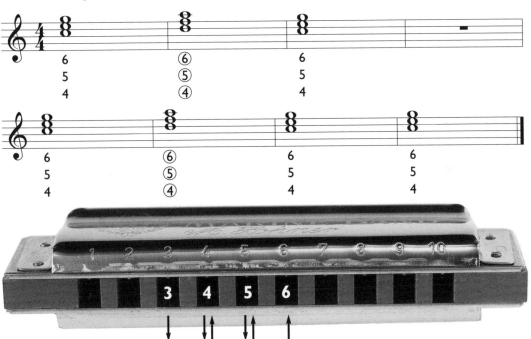

When you're happy with this, try moving from **blowing** ↑**4**, **5**, and **6** to **drawing** ↓**3**, **4**, and **5**.

Use the tip of your tongue, as before, to locate hole 4. Don't take the instrument out of your mouth – you need to learn to sense where you are on the harp without looking. Make sure that your mouth shape does not change, and move the instrument, not your head.

Once you are confident that you can change from 4, 5 and 6 to 3, 4 and 5 with ease, try this, the complete version of the piece you've been working on, which is called "Goin' Around". **Track 7** demonstrates how this should sound.

Track 8 gives you just the backing track without the recorded harmonica. Remember to count for two bars with the 'click' before starting.

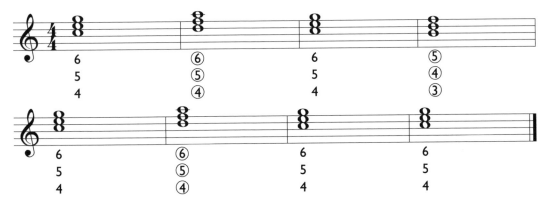

Harmonica notation

You will have noticed by now that each note on the staff corresponds to a number in the tablature. The following diagrams will enable you to see what the name of each note is, where it is on the harmonica, and what it looks like written in music and tablature:

Track 11 demonstrates how it sounds.

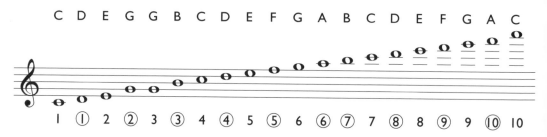

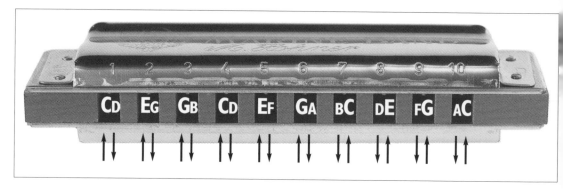

Before we move on, here's some more information about musical notation.

The semibreve note can be divided into two, which produces two notes called *minims*, or half notes, each of which is two beats in length.
Here it is with its rest:

Goin' Around

Now try the full version of "Goin' Around." Listen to **Track 9** to hear how it sounds, then play along with **Track 10**. Don't forget to count!

Another rhythm

Logically enough, minims too can be divided in half, giving us two *crotchets*, or quarter notes, each of which lasts for one beat. Here it is with its rest:

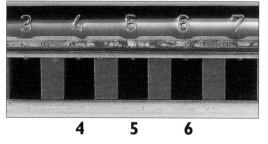

Count: 1   2   3   4   1   2   3   4

Jingle Bells

"Jingle Bells" uses some new note combinations as well as all the note values you have learned so far.

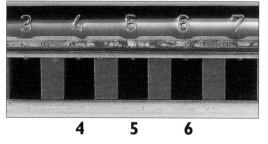

4   5   6   **3   4   5**

To separate the notes, we're going to use a technique called *tonguing*. As you start each note, move your tongue as if you were saying "te" (as in "test"). You will find that this gives a sharper sound to the note than if you begin it in your throat.

Listen to **Track 12** to hear how "Jingle Bells" should sound, and then have a go yourself with **Track 13**.

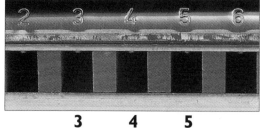

2   3   4

CHECKPOINT

WHAT YOU'VE ACHIEVED SO FAR...

You can now:
* Read specific notes from musical notation and harmonica tablature
* Tell from tablature whether to suck or blow
* Play three-note chords

Jingle Bells

© Copyright 1999 Dorsey Brothers Music Limited, 8/9 Frith Street, London W1.
All Rights Reserved. International Copyright Secured.

Traditional

Two notes only

Now it's time to try to play only two holes at a time, rather than the three you've been using so far.
This is a little bit more tricky, as you're going to have to be more precise.

The easiest way of doing this is to feel with the tip of your tongue for the little upright post between the two holes so as to line it up with the centre of your mouth, then play those holes. Obviously, you should put your tongue away again once you've located the correct position!

Skip To My Lou
In "Skip To My Lou" you should try to separate the quavers using a technique called "double-tonguing". Happily, this does not mean that you have to acquire another tongue from somewhere. Double-tonguing simply means that for the first quaver in a pair you move your tongue as if you were saying "te", and for the second quaver you move your tongue as if you were saying "k" (as in "kite").

Listen to **Track 14**, "Skip To My Lou", and try to follow the score while you listen.

Now try playing along yourself with **Track 15**.

The next piece also introduces a new note value, the *quaver*, or eighth note. These last for half a beat and are counted like this:

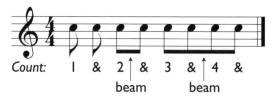

Like all the other note values you've come across, the quaver has an equivalent rest, which looks like this:

Tip
When more than one quaver occurs in a row, they are joined up with a *beam*. This doesn't make any difference to the rhythm of the music – it just makes it easier to read.

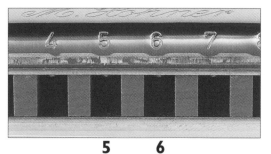

5   6

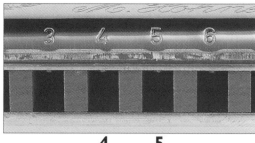

4   5

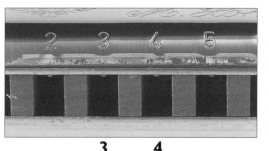

3   4

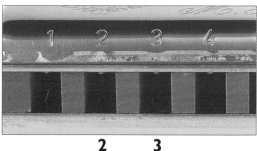

2   3

Skip To My Lou

© Copyright 1999 Dorsey Brothers Music Limited, 8/9 Frith Street, London W1.
All Rights Reserved. International Copyright Secured.

Traditional

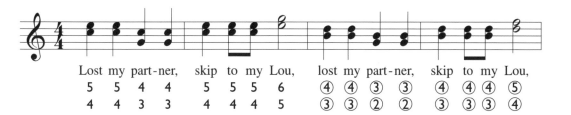

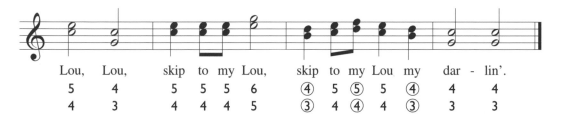

Dotted notes

The next piece introduces a new note value, the *semiquaver*, or sixteenth note, which looks like a quaver but with two little tails instead of one. As you've probably guessed, a semiquaver lasts for a quarter of a beat and is counted like this:

Just like all the other note values, a semiquaver has an equivalent rest, which looks like this:

> ### Tip
>
> Like the quaver, groups of semiquavers can be joined together – this time with a double beam.
> This doesn't affect their duration – it just makes the music easier to read by grouping together notes that belong to the same beat (or beats).

One last point about note values. Any note can have a "dot" added to it which increases its value by half. Thus a dotted semibreve is six beats, a dotted minim equals three beats, a dotted crotchet equals one and a half beats, and so on.

One very common dotted grouping (which you will see in the next tune) is the dotted quaver followed by a single semiquaver. It looks and is counted like this:

The dotted quavers equal three semiquavers, and the single semiquavers at the end round out each beat.

Brown Girl In The Ring
This is the last tune you will play using two-note chords – listen to **Track 16** and then have a go yourself with **Track 17.**

If you have trouble with the faster passages, isolate them and practise them slowly until you can play each pair of notes cleanly. Once you can do that at a slower speed, gradually increase the tempo until you can play along with the audio.

> ### Tip
>
> Use double-tonguing for the groups of quavers.

Brown Girl In The Ring

© Copyright 1999 Dorsey Brothers Music Limited, 8/9 Frith Street, London W1.
All Rights Reserved. International Copyright Secured.

Traditional

Brown girl in the ring, tra - la - la - la - la,
5   5   5 ④ 4   5 ④ 5 ⑤ 6
4   4   4 ③ 3   4 ③ 4 ④ 5

brown girl in the ring, tra - la - la - la - la. Brown girl in the ring,
④ ④ ④ 4 ③ 6 ⑥ 6 ⑤ 5 ④ 5 5 5 ④ 4
③ ③ ③ 3 ② 5 ⑤ 5 ④ 4 ③ 4 4 4 ③ 3

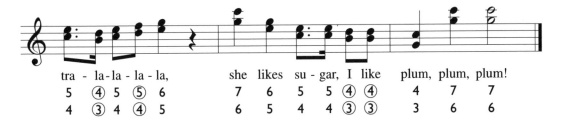

tra - la - la - la - la, she likes su - gar, I like plum, plum, plum!
5 ④ 5 ⑤ 6 7 6 5 5 ④ ④ 4 7 7
4 ③ 4 ④ 5 6 5 4 4 ③ ③ 3 6 6

CHECKPOINT

WHAT YOU'VE ACHIEVED SO FAR...

You can now:
- Read quavers and semiquavers
- Use double-tonguing
- Play two-note chords

Playing single notes

There are several methods of producing one note at a time from the harmonica. We're going to use the *puckering* or *whistle* method. As the name implies, you pucker your lips as if to whistle, making the hole between your lips about the same size as one of those on the instrument. Or you could try imagining that you're drinking a thick milkshake through a straw.

1 Tighten the muscles at the corner of your lips, since the natural lip position is wider and more disposed to sounding full chords – your upper lip should curl up very slightly toward your nose.

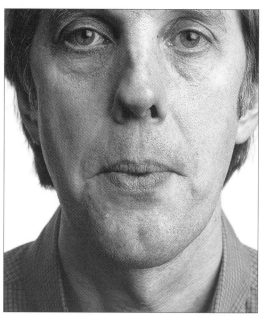

2 Put your upper lip well over the cover of the harp, and your lower lip well under it. The wet inner part of your lips should be in contact with the harmonica, not the dry outer part. This will help to get a good air seal around the mouthpiece, reducing any air loss and promoting not only good tone, but also economical breathing.

3 Blow and draw gently on hole 1. You should find this relatively easy, as there is no number 0 hole to interfere with your efforts!

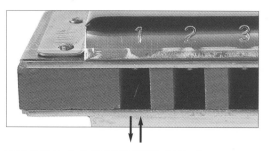

Tip

Remember: the less air you can use, the better – and the longer your harmonica will last!

If you're not sure that you're getting it right, use both your index fingers to cover all the holes except the one you're trying to play. Now play both notes in that hole and try to remember how they sound. Go back to your normal holding position and try to reproduce the sound you made while your fingers were covering the neighbouring holes.

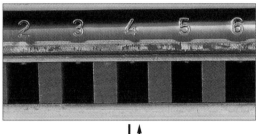

4 Next try hole 4, both blow and draw. Make sure that you are sounding one note and one note only in each breath direction. ,

5 Experiment with all the holes on the instrument, making sure that each note sounds clearly. Be careful with the draw notes in holes 2 and 3 – it is not uncommon for new harp players to have problems with these. Draw 2 should sound the same as blow 3.

Tip

Always remember to move the harmonica across your mouth – don't move your head – it's far less accurate. If you think you're having trouble with this, try practising in front of a mirror.

Stay relaxed and let your breathing be deep, free and easy. When you're happy that you're able to produce single notes clearly, without interference from neighbouring holes and without what is best described as "fuzziness", run through the previous tunes again, but this time play only the top note of each chord shown in the first line of the tablature.

22

When The Saints Go Marching In

Now let's have a go at a piece of classic jazz. The first bar of "When The Saints Go Marching In" has only three beats – this is known as a pick-up bar, and means that the tune starts before the first complete bar. Listen carefully to **Track 18** to see what I mean.

The other thing you haven't encountered before in the music is a tie. This is an arc-shaped line that joins two notes of the same pitch – it means play the first note but sustain it for the length of time indicated by the tied notes.

So, for example, the note G (blow 6) that belongs with the word "saints" at the beginning of the tune is played for 1 semibreve + 1 crotchet = 5 beats.

Listen to **Track 19** to hear how it sounds,

and then try playing along with **Track 20**.

Traditional

© Copyright 1999 Dorsey Brothers Music Limited, 8/9 Frith Street, London W1.
All Rights Reserved. International Copyright Secured.

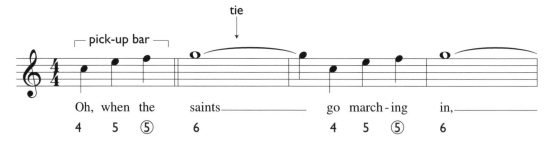

Oh, when the saints go march-ing in,
4 5 ⑤ 6 4 5 ⑤ 6

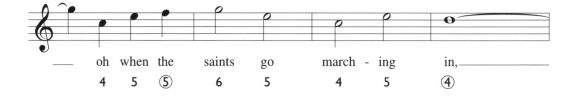

oh when the saints go march - ing in,
4 5 ⑤ 6 5 4 5 ④

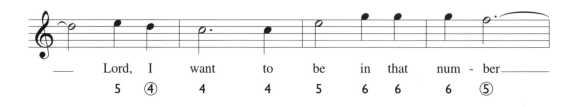

Lord, I want to be in that num - ber
5 ④ 4 4 5 6 6 6 ⑤

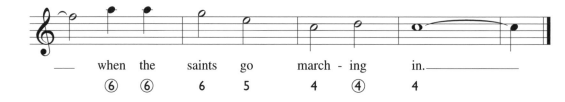

when the saints go march - ing in.
⑥ ⑥ 6 5 4 ④ 4

Down By The Sally Gardens

Here's a lovely Irish melody – make sure you are playing single notes correctly. To hear the melody listen to **Track 21**.

Watch out for the things which look like ties, except they join notes of different pitches. These marks are known as *slurs* and indicate that the notes they join should run into one another, in much the same way as the words in slurred speech. The slurred notes belong to one syllable of the word, so it can help to "sing" the words in your head as you play the tune in order to get these bits right.

You can take advantage of the way the harmonica is laid out when playing some of these slurs. Where the slur covers two notes with the same breath direction in neighbouring holes, only tongue the first note of the pair, and move the harp while maintaining the airflow. The slur will happen almost automatically. Similarly, if the slur involves a change of breath direction, you will get a smoother effect if you only tongue the first note of the pair. Try it!

Now play along with **Track 22**.

© Copyright 1999 Dorsey Brothers Music Limited, 8/9 Frith Street, London W1.
All Rights Reserved. International Copyright Secured.

Traditional

It was down by the Sal - ly— Gar - dens my— love and— I did
4 ④ 5 ④ 4 ④ 5 6 ⑥ 6 7 6 ⑥ 6 5 ④ 4

meet. She— passed the— Sal - ly— Gar - dens with—
4 4 ④ 5 ④ 4 ④ 5 6 ⑥ 6 7 6

lit - tle— snow white feet. She bid me— take love—
⑥ 6 5 ④ 4 4 6 7 ⑦ 6 ⑥ ⑦ 7

ea - sy,— as the leaves grow— on— the— tree, but—
⑦ ⑥ 6 5 6 ⑥ 6 5 6 ⑥ 7 ⑧ 7 4 ④

I was— young and— fool - ish and with her did— not a - gree.
5 ④ 4 ④ 5 6 ⑥ 6 7 6 ⑥ 6 5 ④ 4 4

The Streets Of Laredo

You've now covered the basics of the harmonica – you can play single notes and read harmonica notation and tablature. Now it's time to put your new skills to the test – on the following pages you'll find some popular songs arranged for the harmonica, which will develop your playing even further!

Track 23 The Streets Of Laredo
The next tune sounds great on the harmonica! It has a time-signature of 3/4, otherwise known as waltz time. This means there are only three beats in each bar, rather than the four you're used to – so remember to count 1, 2, 3 / 1, 2, 3 and so on. Try playing along with **Track 24**.

Traditional

© Copyright 1999 Dorsey Brothers Music Limited, 8/9 Frith Street, London W1.
All Rights Reserved. International Copyright Secured.

Annie Laurie

This is a well-known Scottish melody. Watch out for the big jumps from hole 4 to hole 7, and make sure that you are playing them accurately. If necessary isolate that jump and practise it slowly.
Listen to **Track 25**,
then try playing along with **Track 26**.

The tune also makes use of the high register of the harmonica. You will need to keep your throat very open to prevent these notes sounding squeaky, and bear in mind that they require a little less breath and a little more control to get them to sound sweet.

© Copyright 1999 Dorsey Brothers Music Limited, 8/9 Frith Street, London W1.
All Rights Reserved. International Copyright Secured.

Traditional

My Bonnie Lies Over The Ocean

This old favourite again uses the high notes of the harmonica, and is also in waltz time.

Listen to **Track 27**,

and play along with **Track 28**.

Traditional

© Copyright 1999 Dorsey Brothers Music Limited, 8/9 Frith Street, London W1.
All Rights Reserved. International Copyright Secured.

My bon - nie lies ov - er the o - cean,_____ my
6   8   ⑧   7   ⑧   7   ⑥   6   5   6

bon - nie lies ov - er the sea._____ My bon - nie lies
8   ⑧   7   7   ⑦   7   ⑧   6   8   ⑧   7

ov - er the o - cean,_____ oh bring back my
⑧   7   ⑥   6   5   6   ⑥   ⑧   7

bon - nie to me._____ Bring back, oh
⑦   ⑥   ⑦   7   6   7   ⑦

bring back, oh bring back my bon - nie to
⑥   ⑧   7   ⑦   ⑦   ⑦   ⑦   ⑥   ⑦

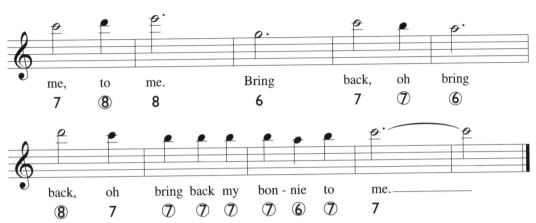

me,	to	me.	Bring	back,	oh	bring
7	⑧	8	6	7	⑦	⑥

back,	oh	bring	back	my	bon - nie	to	me.
⑧	7	⑦	⑦	⑦	⑦	⑥	⑦	7

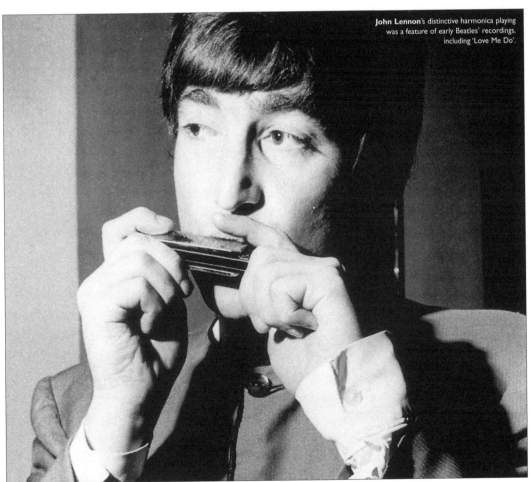

John Lennon's distinctive harmonica playing was a feature of early Beatles' recordings, including 'Love Me Do'.

Twinkle, Twinkle, Little Star

Try to play this gently and quietly. One of the best ways of putting music across is to hold a strong image in your mind of what it is that you are trying to convey. If you can see it, your listeners will too; so with this tune try to imagine the sense of wonder that a child has as it looks up at the stars through the night sky. This children's favourite introduces a new time signature, 2/4. There are only two beats in each bar, so count **1**, **2** – **1**, **2** etc.

Listen to **Track 29** and play along with **Track 30**.

Traditional

© Copyright 1999 Dorsey Brothers Music Limited, 8/9 Frith Street, London W1.
All Rights Reserved. International Copyright Secured.

O Christmas Tree

Track 31 is an arrangement of this well-known carol in 3/4 time – pay particular attention to the dotted quaver/semiquaver pairs.

Track 32 provides the accompaniment for you to play along with.

© Copyright 1999 Dorsey Brothers Music Limited, 8/9 Frith Street, London W1.
All Rights Reserved. International Copyright Secured.

Traditional

O   Christ-mas Tree, O   Christ-mas Tree, you   stand in ver - dant
3   4   4   4   ④   5   5   5   5   ④   5   ⑤   ③

beau - ty!   O   Christ - mas Tree,   O   Christ - mas Tree,   you
④   4   3   4   4   4   ④   5   5   5   5

stand in ver - dant   beau - ty!   Your   boughs are green   in
④   5   ⑤   ③   ④   4   6   6   5   ⑥   6

sum - mer's glow   and   do not fade   in   win - ter's snow.   O
6   ⑤   ⑤   ⑤   ⑤   ④ 6   ⑤   ⑤   5   5   3

Christ - mas Tree, O   Christ-mas Tree, you   stand in ver-dant   beau - ty!
4   4   4   ④   5   5   5   5   ④   5 ⑤ ③   ④   4

Carrickfergus

This arrangement of the traditional Irish melody is also in 3/4 time. Watch out for the slurs here, and try to play them as smoothly as possible. Listen to **Track 33**.

The backing track is on **Track 34**.

Traditional

© Copyright 1999 Dorsey Brothers Music Limited, 8/9 Frith Street, London W1. All Rights Reserved. International Copyright Secured.

Sonny Boy Williamson who played with bands such as The Animals and The Yardbirds, was a master of blues harmonica playing.

The harmonica can bring out a lot of different kinds of emotions

▼ **Paul Jones** "[I decided to learn the harmonica] due to its similarity to the sound of a human being in a high state of emotion"

▼ **Paul Butterfield** "The harmonica can bring out a lot of different kinds of emotions... and feelings..."

The Bluebells Of Scotland

This should not present you with too many difficulties. **Track 35** is the demonstration track.

Track 36 is the backing track.

© Copyright 1999 Dorsey Brothers Music Limited, 8/9 Frith Street, London W1.
All Rights Reserved. International Copyright Secured.

Traditional

O where, tell me where is your— high-land lad-die
6   7   ⑦   ⑥   6   ⑥   ⑦   7   5   5   ⑤   ④

gone?   O   where,   tell   me   where   is   your—
4   6   7   ⑦   ⑥   6   ⑥   ⑦   7

high-land   lad-die   gone?   He's   gone   with   stream-ing
5   5   ⑤   ④   4   6   5   4   5   6

ban - ners, where no-ble deeds are done. And it's
7   ⑥   7   ⑦   6   ⑥   6   6   ⑥   ⑦

oh! In my heart, I_____ wish him safe at home.
7   ⑦   ⑥   6   ⑥   ⑦   7   5   5   ⑤   ④   4

The Yellow Rose Of Texas

The remaining tunes will expand your repertoire without introducing any new techniques or note values.

Listen to **Track 37** for the demo and play along with **Track 38**.

Traditional

© Copyright 1999 Dorsey Brothers Music Limited, 8/9 Frith Street, London W1.
All Rights Reserved. International Copyright Secured.

There's a yel-low rose in Tex-as I'm go-ing home to
6 ⑤ 5 6 6 6 ⑥ 6 ⑤ 5 6 7 ⑧

see, she wants no oth-er fel-low, no-
8 6 6 8 8 8 8 ⑧ 7

bo-dy on-ly me. Oh, she cried so when I
⑦ 7 ⑧ 8 ⑧ 6 ⑤ 5 6 6 6

left her that it near-ly broke my heart, and I
⑥ 6 6 ⑤ 5 6 7 ⑧ 8 6 6

hope that when we meet a-gain we nev-er more will part.
6 ⑨ ⑨ ⑨ ⑨ 8 ⑧ 7 7 6 8 ⑧ 7

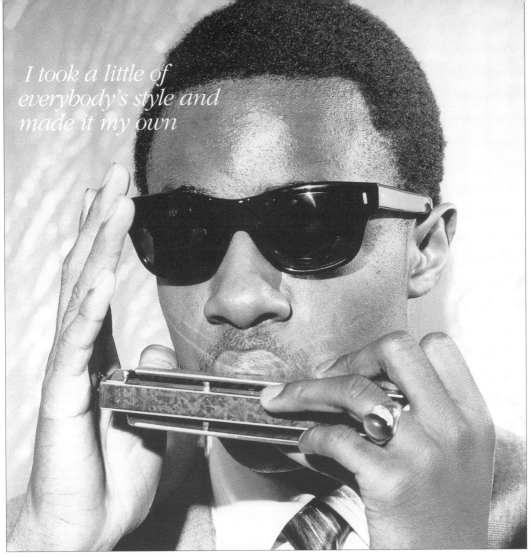

I took a little of everybody's style and made it my own

▲ **Stevie Wonder** featured here playing a chromatic harp, "[When] I started playing the blues... I took a little of everybody's style and made it my own..."

▼ **Lee Oskar:** Began his career with the band War, went solo, and created his own 'signature' harmonica.

◄ **Magic Dick** from the J Geils Band. "My parents gave me a harmonica when I was three years old... and I was just wild about it."

The Leaving Of Liverpool

Track 39 is the demo track.

Track 40 is the backing track.

Traditional

© Copyright 1999 Dorsey Brothers Music Limited, 8/9 Frith Street, London W1.
All Rights Reserved. International Copyright Secured.

So fare thee well my love, my____
7 ⑦ 7 ⑧ ⑦ 6 ⑦ ⑧

own true love, for when I re - turn u -
7 ⑥ 6 4 ④ 5 6 6 6

-ni - ted we will be.____ It's not the
⑥ 6 ⑤ 5 ④ 6 6 ⑤

leav - ing of Li - ver - pool that grieves____ me, but my
5 5 6 ⑤ 5 ④ 4 7 ⑥ 6 4 ④

dar - ling when I think of thee.____
5 6 6 5 ④ 4 4

Congratulations!

I hope that you've enjoyed playing through this book and that you will feel inspired to carry on making music on your harmonica in whichever style most interests you. Feel free to ask other players about their experience and techniques, and remember to have fun. Making music should be an enjoyable experience!

To hear how the pro's do it, check out some recordings by these influential harmonica players:
Jerry Portnoy (Muddy Waters, Eric Clapton)
Lee Oskar
Charlie Musselwaite (John Lee Hooker)
Paul Butterfield (The Butterfield Blues Band)
Brendan Power (Riverdance)
Norton Buffalo (The Steve Miller Band)

John Mayall "The father of British Blues" – his first single, 'Crawling Up A Hill' featured a distorted harmonica and Hammond organ.

Harmonica classics

Now that you've got to grips with the fundamentals of harmonica playing, try listening to how the professionals do it! The songs listed below all feature classic harmonica parts; some are more difficult than others, but armed with the basic techniques you've learnt in this book, you should soon be able to approach some of them.

Good Morning Little School Girl John Mayall
Love Me Do The Beatles
Magic Bus The Who
Midnight Rambler Rolling Stones
Mr Tambourine Man Bob Dylan
The River Bruce Springsteen
There Must Be An Angel Eurythmics (Stevie Wonder)
Heart Of Gold Neil Young

Neil Young

Roger Daltry

Bob Dylan

Bruce Springsteen

Mick Jagger

Further reading

Now you're ready to move onto more advanced material – investigate some of the titles below; they'll help you continue to develop your technique, and will introduce you to some of the great harmonica repertoire that you'll be able to play. See the Music Sales Catalogue for the full list of titles.

Instant Harmonica

The series that gets you playing great music straight away and gives tips on professional techniques and styles.

Instant Harmonica
Book, Cassette and Instrument
AM 73610
Instant Blues Harmonica
Book and Cassette
DH10032
Instant Chromatic Harmonica
Book DH10024
Cassette DH 10078

Rock for Harmonica/ Jazz for Harmonica

Classic rock and jazz hits arranged for harmonica, including 'Take the A Train', 'Satin Doll', 'Riders on the Storm' and 'Three Steps to Heaven'.

Rock for Harmonica
31 great rock classics arranged for Harmonica
Book AM 91946
Jazz for Harmonica
37 all-time great jazz tracks for harmonica.
Book AM91949

Harmonica Power!
Video, with Norton Buffalo

Buffalo's lively, comprehensive course covers the essentials needed for all styles: breathing, tonguing, single-note and chordal playing, bending, vibrato, rhythmic patterns and more.
Harmonica Power! Video One: Norton Buffalo's Bag of Tricks
HSV 602041
Harmonica Power! Video Two: Norton Buffalo's Blues Technique
Video: 90 mins HSV 602030
Harmonica Power! Complete two-tape series
Video: 80 mins HSV 602954

Includes advanced techniques – chord blocking, octave and harmony playing – plus Norton's prescription for "harmonica survival".
A wealth of information!